Our Eternal
Evolution

Vina Mistry

BookLeaf
Publishing

India | USA | UK

Our Eternal Evolution © 2023 Vina Mistry

All rights reserved.

Vina Mistry asserts the moral right to be identified as author of this work.

Presentation by *BookLeaf Publishing*

Web: www.bookleafpub.com

E-mail: info@bookleafpub.com

ISBN: 9789358319002

First edition 2023

DEDICATION

To my younger self, dreams do come true

ACKNOWLEDGEMENT

I thought writing Our Eternal Evolution was going to be easy, one day into writing I realised how wrong I was. The next 21 days were filled with self-doubt, tears and moments of triumph. I wouldn't trade a second of it, as it has been by far the most rewarding experience of my life to date.

I am eternally indebted to my friends and family who supported me through the most difficult period of my life. They have witnesses my personal evolution and have loved me regardless. Without them I don't think I would've been able to move forward and write this book. Thank you to those people, you know who you are.

A special thank you to my secondary school literature teachers, who's passion for the written word inspired me more than they could ever imagine.

Thank you to Book Leaf Publishing, without them my dream to have a published anthology may never have been realised.

Finally, a huge thank you to you, the reader. Thank you for taking the time out of your lives to read these poems that mean so much to me. I am forever grateful.

PREFACE

You and I are the same. Yes, I'm brown and you may not be. I'm a woman and you may not be. I'm 27 and you may not be. But beneath the external differences, you and I are the same. We're human.

This thought was the inspiration behind Our Eternal Evolution. Despite how similar we are, humans cannot resist the urge to wage war, seek out conflict and compete with each other to drain the resources of our planet.

I believe that humanity still has a chance to save the planet that we live on. There are many people out there currently campaigning for the conservation of planet Earth. My hope is that at least one of you reading this book is inspired to travel the world and save as much of it as you can.

The following poems were written to serve as a reminder that the planet is beautiful and that we, like the universe, are ever evolving.

Creation

BANG!
I blinked, struggling to see, to hear, to think
That's when I saw something I'd never seen
before
A light so bright I smiled despite
Despite the fear inside, as rocks collide

SLAM!
Sparks dance and colours form, I see a gemstone
being born
Blues and greens marry together, floating high,
as light as a feather
I watch it spin around as if to say

Hello universe I'm here to stay

Emerald Life

When the dust settled I peered again
Through the clouds I heard the rain
When they parted my core delight
A little green shoot struggling with might

The first splash of colour against the grey
Oh, how I wish you were there that day
I weeped at the beauty I knew was to unfold
Wondered at the stories yet to be told

One green shoot turned to two then three
Jungles form and blossom over centuries
A turquoise blue ribbon ran through the land
An iridescent cake topped with sea and sand

With eyelids heavy I closed them to sleep
As I did I heard the first echos sheep

Breath of Life

Birdsong bounces over the horizon
American plains overflow with bison
Sapphire ripples lap coasts on this sphere
I can smell the salt from up here!

It's been millennia since I've seen
A planet with so much life it teems
Tulips, roses, flowers alike
Are visited by bees, pollinated by flight

The Luna orchestrates the tide
While wolves call to it on mountain side
Creatures walk, crawl, glide and fly
All live in harmony, no cruelty, no lies

I startled awake
The ground beneath began to shake

The Beast Below

Maples scream and oaks bow
Fear walks my bones and vultures crow
Thunder echos but not from the sky
I think you'd agree nows a good time to cry

Bravery born I look below
From within, rivers of tears do flow
A green land once so pure
Is now crimson, red with gore

Dinosaurs!
The largest beasts I've ever seen
Tearing meat from bones that gleen
Badgers burrow and hide from sight
Birdsong whispers, afraid to take flight

WHOOSH!
Blazing light streams past
I yell down, "run fast"!
Rocks collide, cavities form
Volcanoes bleed, hot liquid storms

The mighty beasts scream and perish
Silence dawns, eerie and hellish

Prometheus

We danced around the sun as I slept
Round and around and around again
Years went by and time it crept
Until one day a cry pierced the rain

Looking down i was shocked to see
A tiny person, a human being
It took a step then two then three
Marveling at the emerald sight it's seeing

Pure and ind it helped a bee
That had fallen into a river stream
A spark of hope lit inside of me
That this planet could thrive, not just in a dream

Tiny people grew and grew
began to speak and laugh and learn
Multiplying into villages to
A spark appeared the moods turn

Disaster, they've discovered wood burns

Start of the End

Over time wood turned to clay
Forest shrunk to make some space
The homes they built were here to stay
I've seen elephants with more grace

Over time clay turned to timber
Forest replaced by farming land
Birds and foxes died or injure
Humanity grew, scattered like sane

Over time chins were placed
On certain people from the human race
Unease grew I prepared and braced
For what this planet was about to face

Chained

Years trickles past, with no change
In fact it got worse, the hurt the pain
People bought at auction were all the range
Resistance was met by flogs in the rain

Children ripped from arms of mothers
Fields of cotton reddened with blood
Escaping plantations under nights cover
So many tears, hope drowned in a flood

Just when i thought humanity was doomed
They fought long and hard with tears
Rebel groups came forth and bloomed
Braving the hate despite all their fears

The chains that bound were no longer physical
Morphing into where to sit on a bus
Morphing into which bathroom was permissible
Who thought pigment would cause all this fuss

A New Dawn

Starlight trapped caged in glass
I think I heard them call it a bulb
Factories soon sold this magic en masse
They used it to read and at night to lull

Next came a device to track rotations
I think i heard them call it a clock
Hung up in homes and stations
Time flew by like a flock

Vehicles grew thanks to Ford
Black cars replaced the horse
The divide grew between pauper and Lord
The rich got richer with no remorse

Fields that once enslaved now bloomed
Tractors gave food to the nation
Development began, lady's well-groomed
The rich danced with elation

Abundance

The boom happened and wealth expanded
Time birthed luxury cars and mansions
The wealthy took tours of canyons
Money trees only were planted

Dresses made of diamond and emerald
Sat atop sculpted porcelain dolls
From four to two feet, humanity evolves
But they still permit the poor to tremble

From high up here I can't help but to see
Everything good, bad and brave
Wealth attracts what the poor crave
To be warm and safe, to just be

Diamond Skies

Banquet tables dressed to the max
Hands and necks donned with gems
While plants outside rot from the stems
They eat caviar, peaches and sweet snacks

Private jets, tsunamis of glam
Twirling under a blanket of stars
Humans even came up here to Mars
Their world like a pearl in a clam

Honey flows from all around
Sweet nectar that abundance demand
Earth must provide, maintain this dreamland
I see their future, all burnt to the ground

The poor won't stand to slave like before
I smell it in the air
The unrest we know is there
Here it comes, war, war, war

Dance of the Classes

Classes differ no teachers are found
Poor have bread, water and the street
The rich have land, fruit and meat

Wealth and War

The death of a Tsar and chaos ensue
Conscription gave the poor a cause
A chance to die just because
Families destroyed, tears scattered like dew

Arms are sold to friend and foe
Gold is mined and oil sold
Money made is empty and cold
Hatred spreads, they reap what they sow

Infernos engulf red rivers flow
The dawn of war fast approach
Humans hunt each other and poach
The land of its life its ability to grow

Like pirates at sea, they plunder the Earth
Gutting it alive with dynamite
I hear it scream, my resources are finite
It'll be too late when they see its worth

Ash and Ruin

Amazon once thriving is now dry and cracked
Animals scatter, homeless and die
Giant diamonds in the Arctic collapse
Turn to floods no arc in sight

Needle inserted and oil extracted
Until there's nothing left, shriveled and dying
Lush ground turns to ash and ruin
Food catches fire, starvation follows

Rains turn streets to rivers of pain
Washing away homes, trees and children
The sun catches fire to all below
Lava rays crawl across the floor

I hoped I'd never see
The death of a sibling, a planet like me
There's nowhere to turn, I can't look away
I guess Earth isn't here to stay

Cosmic Conversations

Can you hear me, I want to help
Warn them of the pain you've felt
Cause tsunamis, sirens that ring
Shake your ground, yell and sing

Can you see me, I want to cry
Seeing you struggle and them deny
Bleeding you dry with no thought
That your core isn't blazing red anymore

Piles of gold and oil and ore
Are not enough, they scrounge you for more
Why can't they share life with you
Instead of using and abusing each other to

Your light is fading, snuffed out cold
I can hear your magma, slow as stone
I hear your crust snap and breach
How much more can you take?

Spherical Coffin

Air gets thick, a noose knot tied
Around the neck of humanity and animals alike
Mother Earth fought with might
But you've bled her for the last time

I wish I could say miracles happen
A happy ending is bound to occur
But this isn't a fairy-tale of hope and bloom
It's a reality check, will it inspire change in turn

As a gaze down, Earth once wild and free
Is in shackles, drained, I wish I couldn't see
The skin cracking, molten blood seeping through
A ship sinking along with it's crew

Goodbye my friend, I wish you could stay
Maybe you'll be reborn, sometime, someday

Chrysalis

BOOM!

A crack rings out and she is gone
Life lost, deserted and cold
Dust settles and my tears dry up
What am i meant to do now?

I watches her birth and guided her
Over the years she grew, had life of her own
Life killed her spark, she vanished
Like a mother, sacrificing all she had

WAIT!

What is that I see?
A flaming arrow as straight as can be
Flying out from Earth towards me
Metallic life raft I think that's what it is

Reaching out, desperate to connect
I feel what I thought I never would again
Two by two they lay, incubated, safe
Ready... to try again

Adam and Eve

With a sniper eye I track the pod
Like a fisherman hunts for cod
I see it travel far away
It doesn't slow down, it knows the way

After many years it slows, then stops
Hovers, hesitates, it peers down at the rocks
Anchor loose, it lowers itself down
Silence bellows as it hits the ground

Clam mouth opens inside I look
Rows of pearls in every nook
Hatching forth, they open wide
Curiosity kills this cat and I look inside

Humans crawl like sea creatures did to land
Wobbling slightly but they begin to stand
Looking around at this new lush green world
Eyes wide as huge trees unfurl

It's been years since they've seen
A planet with so much life, so much green
My hope this time is that they learn
From some damage you cannot return

Fairy-tale of Earth

Just like before one rescues a bee
Flailing in water from falling off a tree
This small act gives me floods of hope
This time it'll be different, they've learnt the
ropes

A brand new planet, Earth's sister star
I wonder, I wonder, who you are
I wish you could've met her, my Earth
Or seen her wonders, like Paris or Perth

You'll have new stories to tell
Of how you thrived not how you fell
Humans are really not all bad
They're not destroyers they're just sad

Waters crystal, untouched and pure
Fairy-tale land only heard in lore
Blooms of flowers line the ground
Warmth floods my soul, rings of hope sound

Historic Chains

It's been centuries since we last spoke
Humanity thrives as strong as an oak
Hearts pulse brave and true
Villages raise children, sky's so blue

Something catches the corner of my eye
Fear turns me cold, faith becomes dry
Glinting in the distance a metallic shine
I pray it's not a chain, please be a dime

I see a whip, hear a cry
It's happening again, please God why
Light snuffed out, gone the trust I had
Why is this happening again, it's so sad

People in chains it's dejavu
Children torn from arms of mothers to
History repeats on a different plain
The clouds appear, then the rain

Death and Bird Song

I haven't looked down in years and years
Disappointment takes hold, so do my fears
Breath hitches as I look down
Every face donned a frown

She's being drained her oil her gold
Her diamonds and pearls are sold
Again the rich lavish and gleam
While the poor scavenge and squeam

Hearts sync with the planet below
I feel her dying, losing her glow
There's no life boat in this desert
No way out of the coming unpleasant

All I know is long after they're gone
This planet will thrive, birds will song

Milton Keynes UK
Ingram Content Group UK Ltd.
UKHW021446140424
441120UK00005B/11